I'M A FUTURE
BUG EXPERT!
Written By
Manisha Nayak
Illustrated By
Eliz Ong
AF740838
WS Education
NEW JERSEY · LONDON · SINGAPORE · GENEVA · BEIJING · SHANGHAI · TAIPEI · CHENNAI

Published by
WS Education Pte. Ltd.
5 Toh Tuck Link, Singapore 596224

National Library Board, Singapore Cataloguing in Publication Data
Name(s): Nayak, Manisha. | Ong, Eliz, illustrator.
Title: I'm a future bug expert! / written by Manisha Nayak ; illustrated by Eliz Ong.
Other Title(s): I'm a future scientist!
Description: Singapore : WS Education, [2026]
Identifier(s): ISBN 978-981-98-1046-8 (hardcover) | 978-981-98-1047-5 (paperback) | 978-981-98-1048-2 (book for institutions) | 978-981-98-1049-9 (book for individuals)
Subject(s): LCSH: Entomology--Juvenile literature. | Entomologists--Juvenile literature. | Entomology--Vocational guidance--Juvenile literature.
Classification: DDC 595.7--dc23

British Library Cataloguing-in-Publication Data
A catalogue record for this book is available from the British Library.

Desk Editor: Daniele Lee

Printed in Singapore

CONTENTS

Say 'Hello' to Belle!

Have you ever felt bugged by bugs? These tiny critters can be found everywhere around us. Whether you find them frightening or interesting, they sure are fascinating little creatures.

In science, the term 'bugs' refers to certain insects with piercing mouthparts, such as aphids and bedbugs. However, in everyday language, 'bugs' and 'creepy-crawlies' are commonly used to describe animals that have at least six legs, such as ants, butterflies, spiders and centipedes.

Read on and get to know all about the brilliant world of bugs!

All the best! Belle

Let's Debug Bugs!

Bugs can be found everywhere around you. You can find them at home, in school and even on your way to school! Horrifyingly, some of them may even be living on your bodies!

Let's take a close look at some types of bugs.

Interesting insects

Most often, when we say 'bugs', we're referring to insects. Some common examples are ants, houseflies, mosquitoes, cockroaches, beetles, butterflies and honeybees.

Insects are animals that have six legs. They don't have bones, but they have a hard outer body covering called an exoskeleton. Their bodies have three main segments — the head, the thorax and the abdomen. Some insects also have one or two pairs of wings.

Amazing arachnids

Arachnids, such as spiders, are also commonly referred to as 'bugs'. Arachnids have eight legs and no wings. They have an exoskeleton and their bodies have two main segments.

Mysterious myriapods

The word 'myriapod' comes from ancient Greek and means 'countless feet'. Centipedes and millipedes are the most widely known myriapods.

Myriapods have an exoskeleton. They have multiple body segments and no wings. Most of the segments have a pair of legs. However, some myriapods, like millipedes, have two pairs of legs per segment.

Terrific Transformation

Ever wondered how a caterpillar transforms into a beautiful winged butterfly? Let's take a closer look at the life cycle of a butterfly!

Egg

Female butterflies lay their eggs on plants, usually on the underside of leaves.

Adult

The pupal case breaks open and a beautiful butterfly emerges.

Larva

Each egg hatches into a larva, also known as a caterpillar. The larva looks like a worm and spends most of its time eating.

Watch the transformation here!

Life cycle of a butterfly

Pupa

The larva develops into a pupa, which does not move or feed. It is undergoing a fascinating transformation.

Mix and Match

Bugs come in all shapes and sizes. Can you match these unusual bugs to their names correctly? Psst... their names should give you a hint!

Bug		Name
(a)		Orchid mantis
(b)		Giraffe weevil
(c)		Scorpion fly
(d)		Poodle moth

Hide-and-seek

In the wild, animals need to find food and protect themselves from predators. One of the cleverest ways to do this is to blend into the background and become practically invisible! This is known as camouflage.

Let's take a look at some bugs that have mastered the art of camouflage!

No prizes for guessing why the **orange oakleaf butterfly** is also known as the dead leaf butterfly! This Asian butterfly looks exactly like a dry leaf.

The **common baron caterpillar** is a master of camouflage.
It uses its colour, texture and the yellow line on its back to disguise itself completely against a leaf. This makes it nearly impossible to be spotted.

The **brimstone moth caterpillar** can camouflage itself against a plant such that it looks exactly like a twig. Now that's one clever way to fool your enemies!

A **leaf insect** is able to mimic a leaf so effectively that its predators can't tell the difference. Even when walking, the insect rocks back and forth, exactly like a leaf moving in the wind.

The **goldenrod crab spider** sits on flowers and waits to ambush unsuspecting prey.
It can change its body colour from white to yellow to match the flower it sits on.

The **conehead mantis** is a type of praying mantis. Its colours and shape help it to mimic dead plants and blend completely into its surroundings.

Which other animals use camouflage to find food and hide from their enemies?

Let's Get Rolling!

You may have read about or seen pictures of the dung beetle. It is well known for rolling large, spheres of animal dung with its hind legs, while its head stays close to the ground! Why exactly do these beetles roll dung around? Let's find out!

Dung beetles are insects that collect and feed on the dung of other animals. The dung provides them with nutrients. Rolling the dung into balls makes it easier for the beetles to transport them to a safe area for storage and future use.

Some dung beetles can pull dung balls weighing more than a thousand times their body weight. That's like an average human pulling six double-decker buses full of people!

Watch the dung beetle in action!

Female beetles also use the dung balls to lay eggs. This ensures an immediate supply of food for the larvae when they hatch.

Did You

The word 'centipede' means '100 legs', but no centipede species has ever been found with exactly 100 legs! That's because centipedes always have an odd number of leg pairs. Centipedes can have 10 to roughly a few hundred legs.

Most spiders have eight eyes!

Know?

Ants can typically carry 10-50 times their own body weight. Some species can carry even more!

If you thought all beetles were tiny, think again! The rhinoceros beetle is one of the largest beetles in the world. It can grow up to 15 cm long!

Fleas don't have wings, but they're great at jumping. Some types of fleas can jump up to 200 times their body length!

Some types of lice can live in beards, eyebrows and even eyelashes!

When honeybees find a good source of food, they do a special dance to tell the other bees in their hive about it. The dance, known as the waggle dance, indicates the distance and direction of the food source from the hive.

Pond skaters are insects with specialised legs that allow them to walk on the surface of water without sinking!

Butterflies use their feet to taste! They use taste sensors located on their feet to determine if a plant is suitable for their caterpillars to eat.

Spider silk is a protein fibre spun by spiders to make their webs. Spider silk can be up to five times stronger than a steel thread of the same size!

Observe this spider spin a web!

The Travel Bug

Except what?
I was badly bitten.
Bitten?? Bitten by what??

Bed bugs! Look!
Oh, those look bad!
Where and how did this happen?
I think the hotel bed had bed bugs. They bit me in my sleep.

Later that day...
I'm so sorry to hear that Shaun was bitten by bed bugs during his holiday.
Dad, I'm feeling paranoid now. We're going on holiday next week!
What if our hotel room has bed bugs too?

Don't worry. While it's true that bed bugs are commonly found in many hotels, we can take certain precautions.
I'm wondering what bed bugs are doing in hotels anyway!
Maybe they're on holiday too!

Bed bugs are tiny insects that feed on blood.
Bed bugs are common in hotels as there is a constant inflow of people and their luggage.
Bed bugs and their eggs are tiny. They can get into clothing, furniture and luggage. They are also easily transported when travellers move from hotel to hotel.

What can we do to avoid running into bed bugs during our holiday?
Well, the first thing we always do before booking a hotel is check its reviews.
HOTEL U
BED BUG ALERT!
SCARY!! BED BUGS IN HOTEL...
That's right! If any reviews mention bed bugs, we avoid booking that hotel.

However, we still need to be alert. After we check into our hotel, we should check the room carefully for bed bugs.
How do we spot them? They're so tiny!
I'll show you when we reach our hotel.

One week later...
All right, let's check for bed bugs!
Let's start with the bed. Look out for flat and reddish-brown insects that are about the size of an apple seed.
In addition to live insects, we should also look out for any dark spots as that could be bed bug poop.
BED BUG POOP

You might also be able to spot bed bug eggs or outer coverings shed by bed bugs.
Their usual hiding places are in furniture, drawers, cupboards, and other nooks and crannies in the room.
All clear!
Yay! We can sleep in peace with no bed bugs to bug us!
The end

Magical Moulting

Insects have a hard outer body covering known as the exoskeleton. As an insect grows, its exoskeleton becomes too small for it and must be shed. The periodic shedding of the exoskeleton and growing of a new and larger exoskeleton is known as moulting.

A cicada moulting

Insects cannot survive without their protective exoskeleton. This means that they need to construct their new exoskeleton while they're inside the old one! When the new exoskeleton is ready, the old one splits open. The insect sheds the old exoskeleton and continues to expand the new one. The new exoskeleton hardens and darkens, making the insect look like itself again!

Caterpillars moulting

Millipedes and spiders need to moult too.

A millipede moulting

A spider moulting

Many other animals also shed their outer covering and grow new ones. Examples are snakes, lizards, frogs and birds!

Detective Work

The pictures below are close-up shots of the eyes of different bugs. Can you identify them correctly?

Find the answers on page 55!

I'm Inspired

Once upon a time, people believed that living things could arise on their own from non-living things such as air and mud. This was known as 'spontaneous generation'. However, in later years, research and experiments disproved this belief.

Maria Sibylla Merian was a scientist who contributed greatly to disproving the idea of spontaneous generation. Let's find out more about her!

WORD WHIZ

spontaneous: done in a way that is natural, often sudden, and not planned or forced

Born in 1647 in Germany, Maria was keenly interested in insects from a very young age. She began to observe and illustrate caterpillars, moths and butterflies in great detail. She published several books in which she depicted the life cycles of insects.

Her work contributed significantly towards disproving the belief that insects were spontaneously generated from decaying matter such as rotting fruit or meat. The aesthetic quality of her artworks also helped raise the standards of scientific illustrations.

Maria's illustration showing the various stages in the life cycle of the giant sphinx moth

Freaky Fungus

Look at the picture carefully. What's that growing out of the ant's head? It's actually a mind-controlling fungus at work!

The zombie ant fungus is notorious for hijacking the body and mind of insects such as ants. Let's find out more!

mind.

WORD WHIZ

spore: a tiny structure by which living things such as fungi reproduce

Holding complete control of the helpless ant's mind, the fungus forces the ant to move to a location that would be suitable to distribute spores. Once it reaches the location, the ant locks its jaws around a leaf and simply waits for its death. After the ant dies, the fungus causes a long stalk to grow through the ant's head. The spores in the stalk are released, ready to infect more ants and continue the cycle. Freaky, isn't it?

Watch the 'zombie' ants here!

True or False?

Do you remember what you have learnt about bugs so far? Test yourself with this quiz! Which sentences are true and which are false?

1. The legs of an insect are found on the abdomen.
2. Spiders have eight legs.
3. The larva of a butterfly does not feed.
4. Dung beetles eat dung.
5. Centipedes have 100 legs.
6. Butterflies taste with their feet.
7. Spider silk is stronger than steel.
8. Bed bugs can only be seen under a microscope.
9. Insects shed their outer covering during moulting.
10. The zombie ant fungus can control the mind of its victims.

Find the answers on page 55!

Project Work

The mealworm beetle is a type of insect. It has four stages in its life cycle — egg, larva (commonly known as mealworm), pupa and adult.

In this project, we will observe some stages in the life cycle of a mealworm beetle!

What you need

- Two plastic containers with lids
- Mealworms (you can buy them at a pet shop)
- Oatmeal
- Potatoes or apples
- Paper towels
- An adult to supervise

What you need to do

1. Get the help of an adult to poke small holes in the lids of the containers so that your mealworms have enough air to breathe.

2. Line the base of one container with the oatmeal. This will be the primary food for your mealworms. Gently place the mealworms in the container and close the lid.

3. Place pieces of potatoes or apples in the container regularly. The moisture in them will provide your mealworms with water.

4. Once the mealworms develop into pupae, they will stop feeding and move very little. Transfer the pupae into the other container lined with a paper towel so that they can develop undisturbed.

5. Once the adult beetles emerge, they can be transferred back to the first container as they eat the same food as the mealworms. The adults are ready to continue the life cycle!

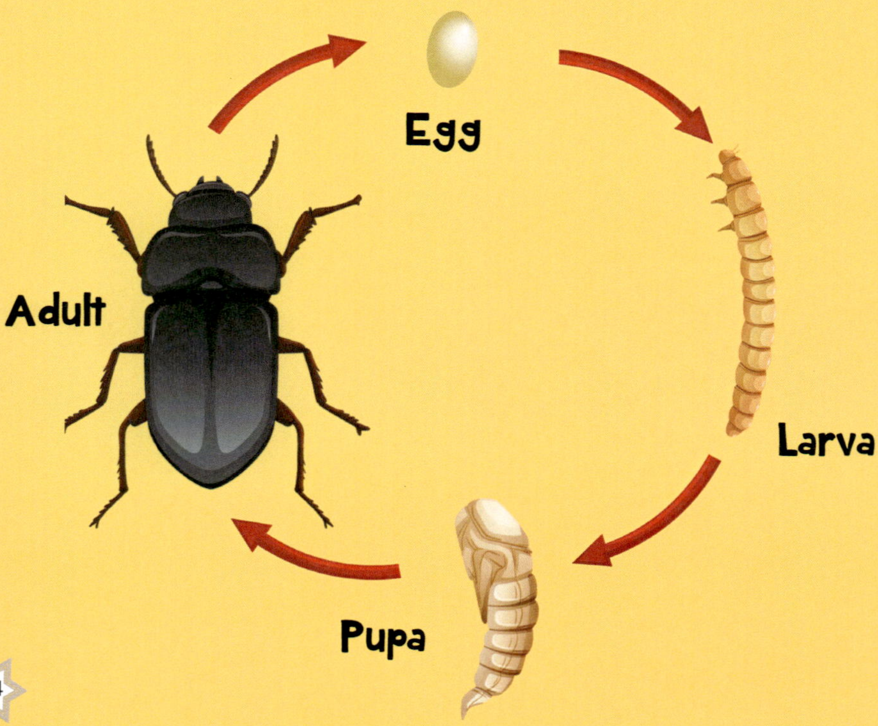

Answers

Mix and Match (page 12)

(a) Scorpion fly

(b) Orchid mantis

(c) Poodle moth

(d) Giraffe weevil

Detective Work (page 44)

(a) Spider

(b) Centipede

(c) Bed bug

(d) Praying mantis

(e) Cockroach

(f) Mosquito

(g) Honeybee

(h) Ladybug

True or False? (page 51)

1.	False	2.	True
3.	False	4.	True
5.	False	6.	True
7.	True	8.	False
9.	True	10.	True

I'M A FUTURE SCIENTIST!

The *I'm a Future Scientist!* series of full-colour books for 6–12 year olds will spark sustained interest in scientific fields, such as botany, zoology, marine biology, conservation and the environment, astronomy, and many more, delivering primary-school-level Science learning points in an engaging and relatable way! Through clearly written educational articles, fun cartoons, suggested hands-on activities, as well as full-colour photographs and illustrations, these books are the perfect companions for budding scientists to delve further into a wide range of scientific fields.

WS Education

Email sales@wspc.com for sales enquiries and bulk purchase opportunities.